I0483617

# ArtLife

Created and Illustrated by:

## Kelly Kristin Ballantine

Copyright 2017 Kelly Kristin Ballantine
All rights reserved.

ISBN-13: 978-0692891353

ISBN-10: 0692891358

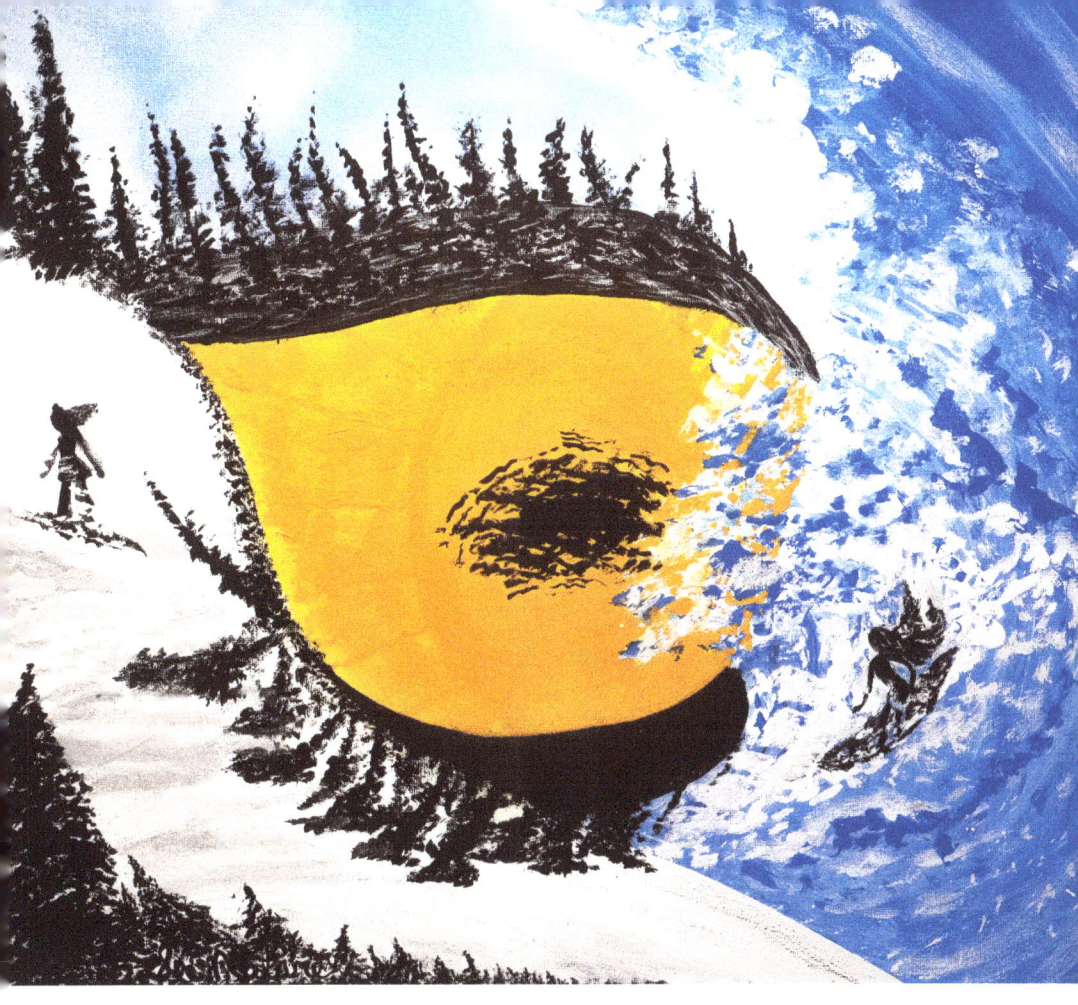

## Intent

ArtLife is dedicated to those emitting or pursuing positive vibrations throughout the universe. This short story was created to showcase works of art while inspiring creativity and love. It is for those who want to be happy and live a happy life. Enjoy art while a beautiful yet simplistic story comes to life. Peace and love to all, and don't forget to create!

*Art is love!*

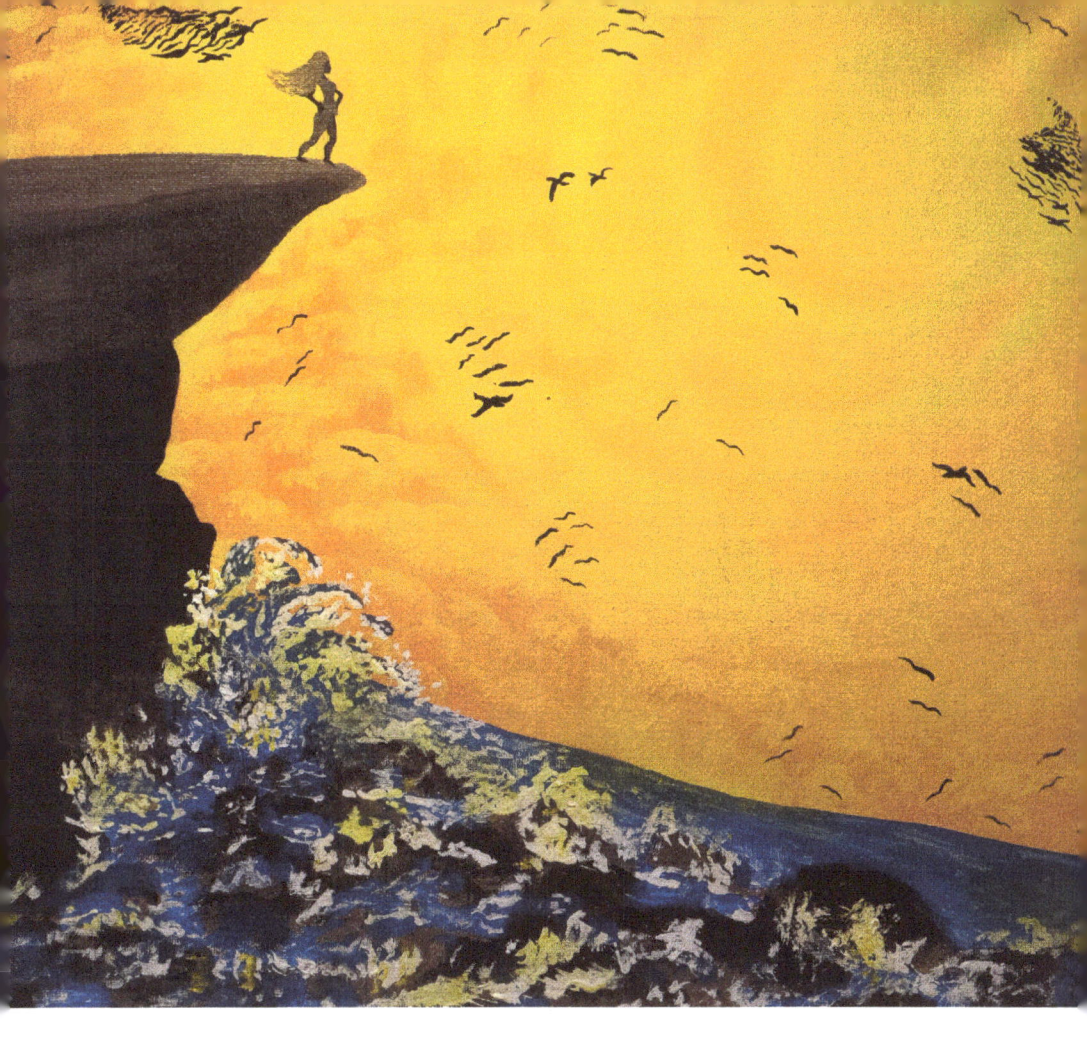

*She needed some time to be reflective so she could conquer her unknown objective.*

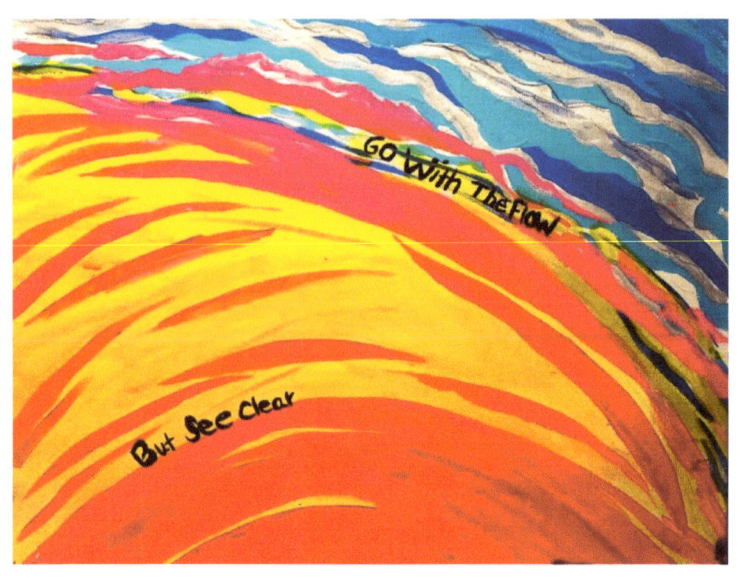

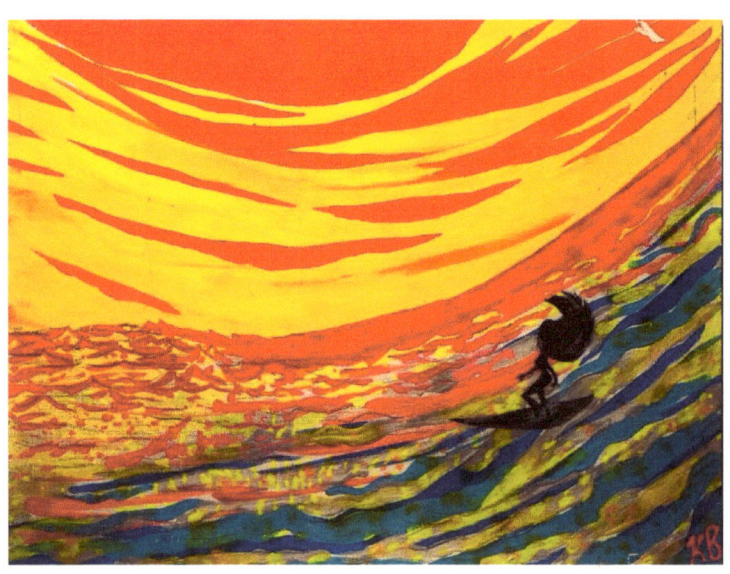

*She pondered in a bewildered*
*state of amazement.*

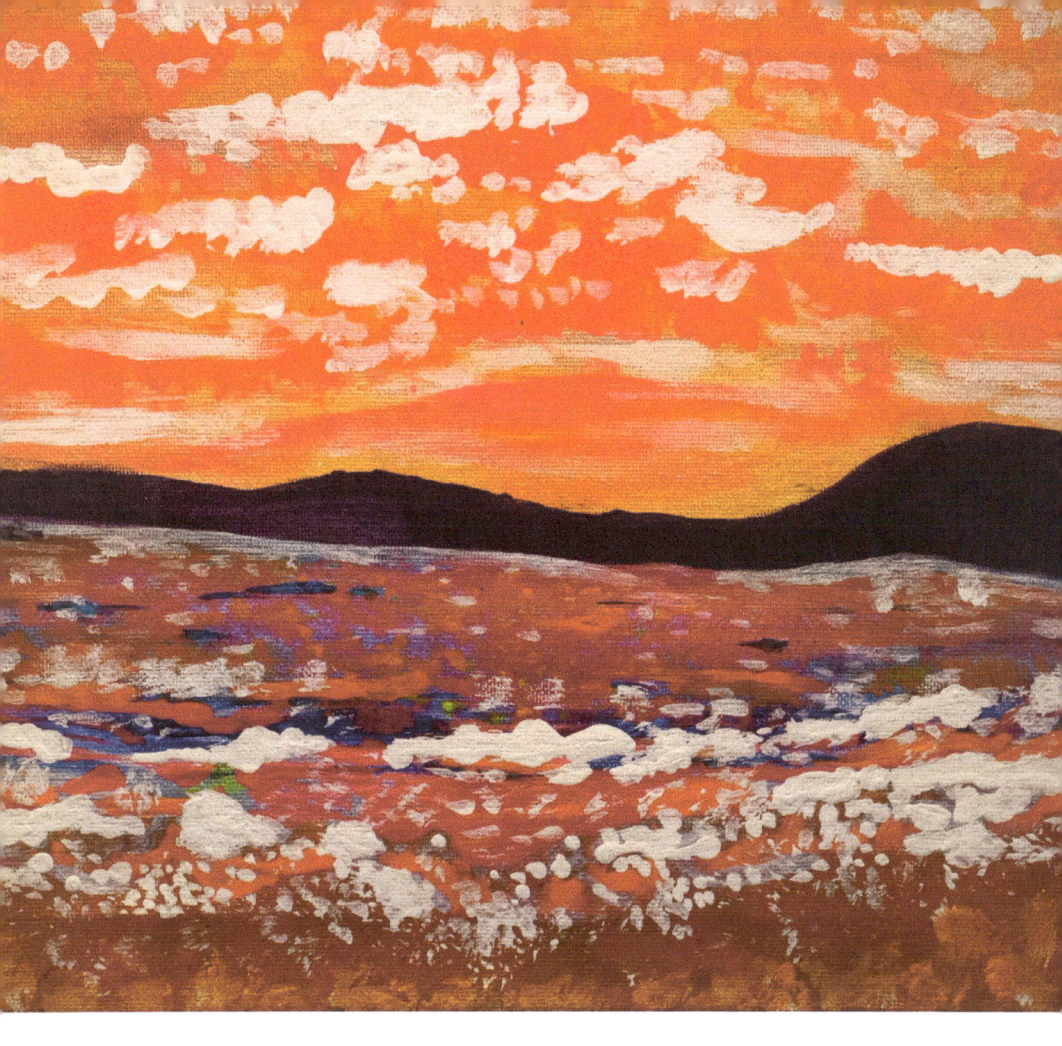

She wandered through the day in
wonder of her life's path. She
questioned everything and couldn't
just be. She often thought, "To
think so much, why me?"

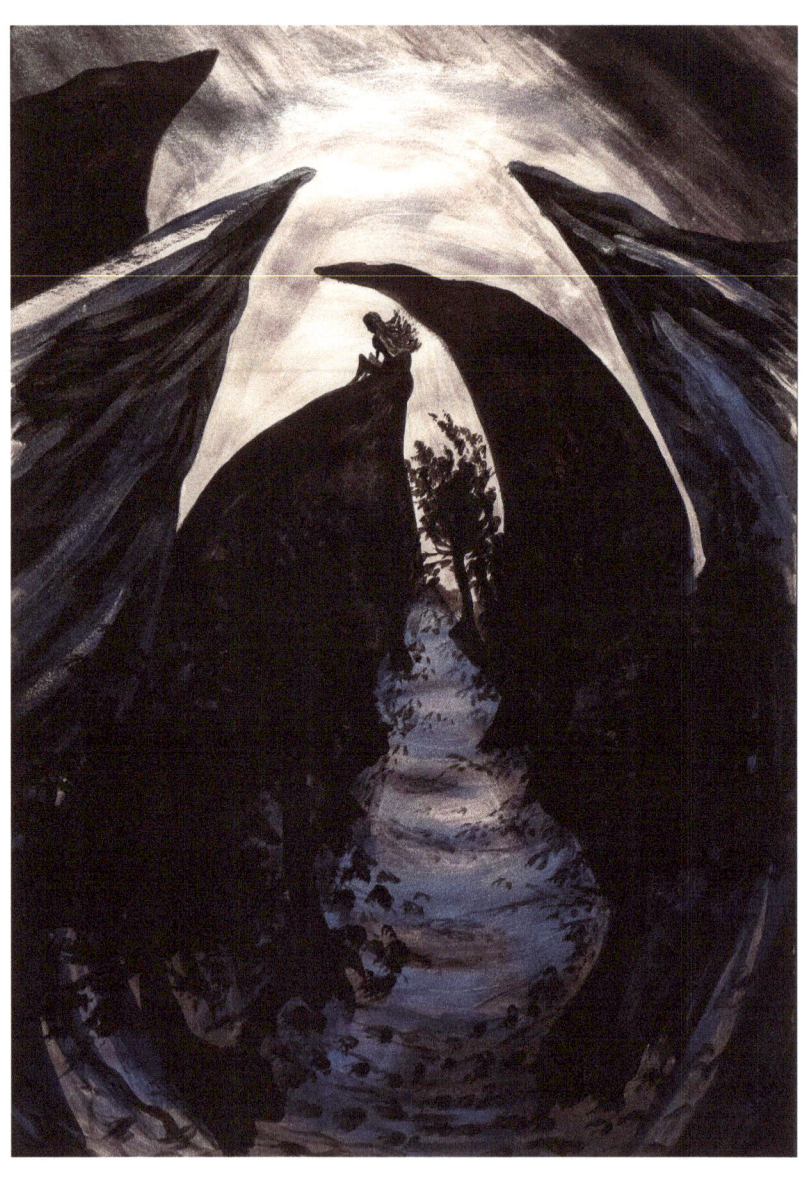

*She sat alone in the quiet of the night,*
*searching for answers where there*
*was no daylight.*

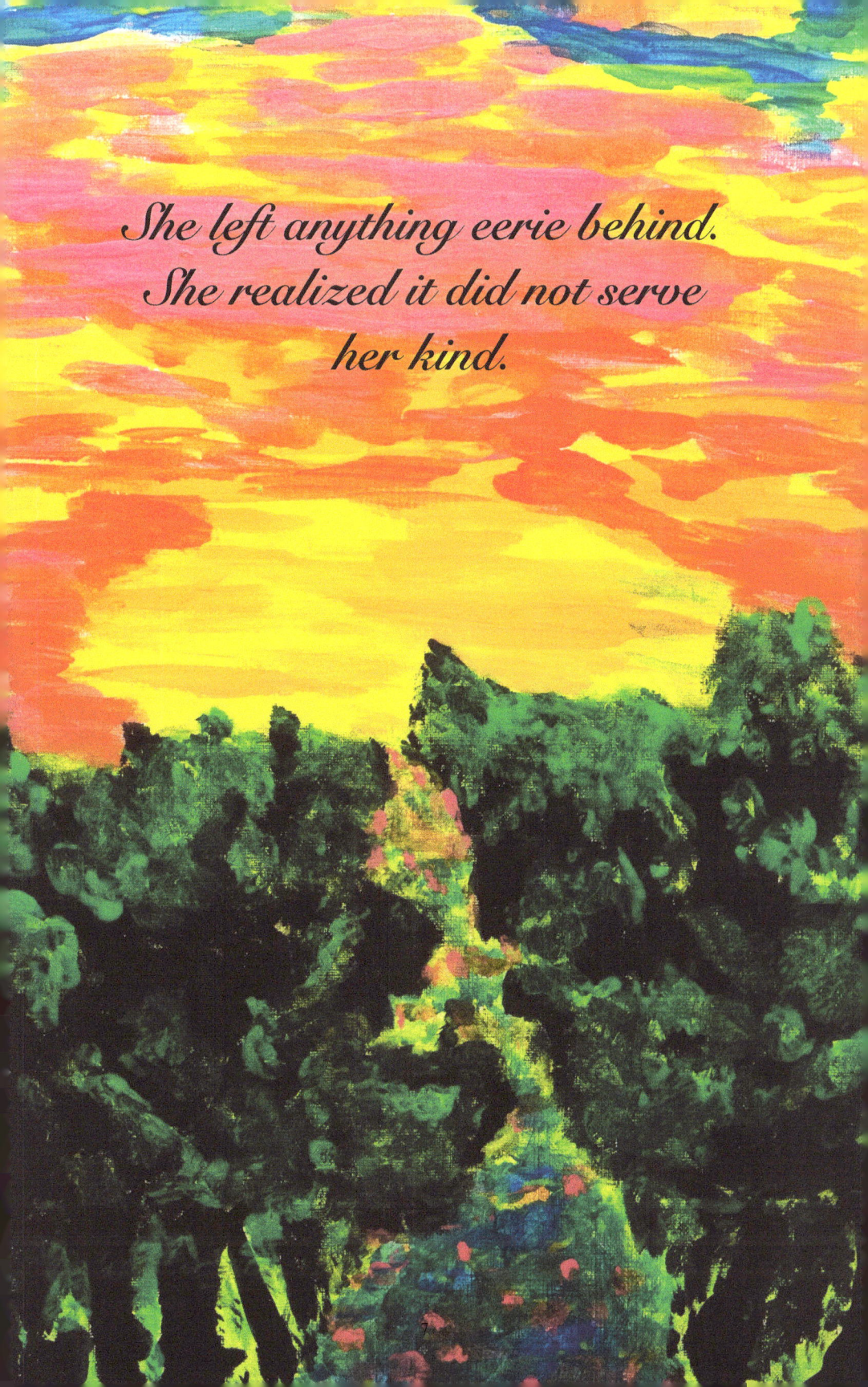

She left anything eerie behind.
She realized it did not serve
her kind.

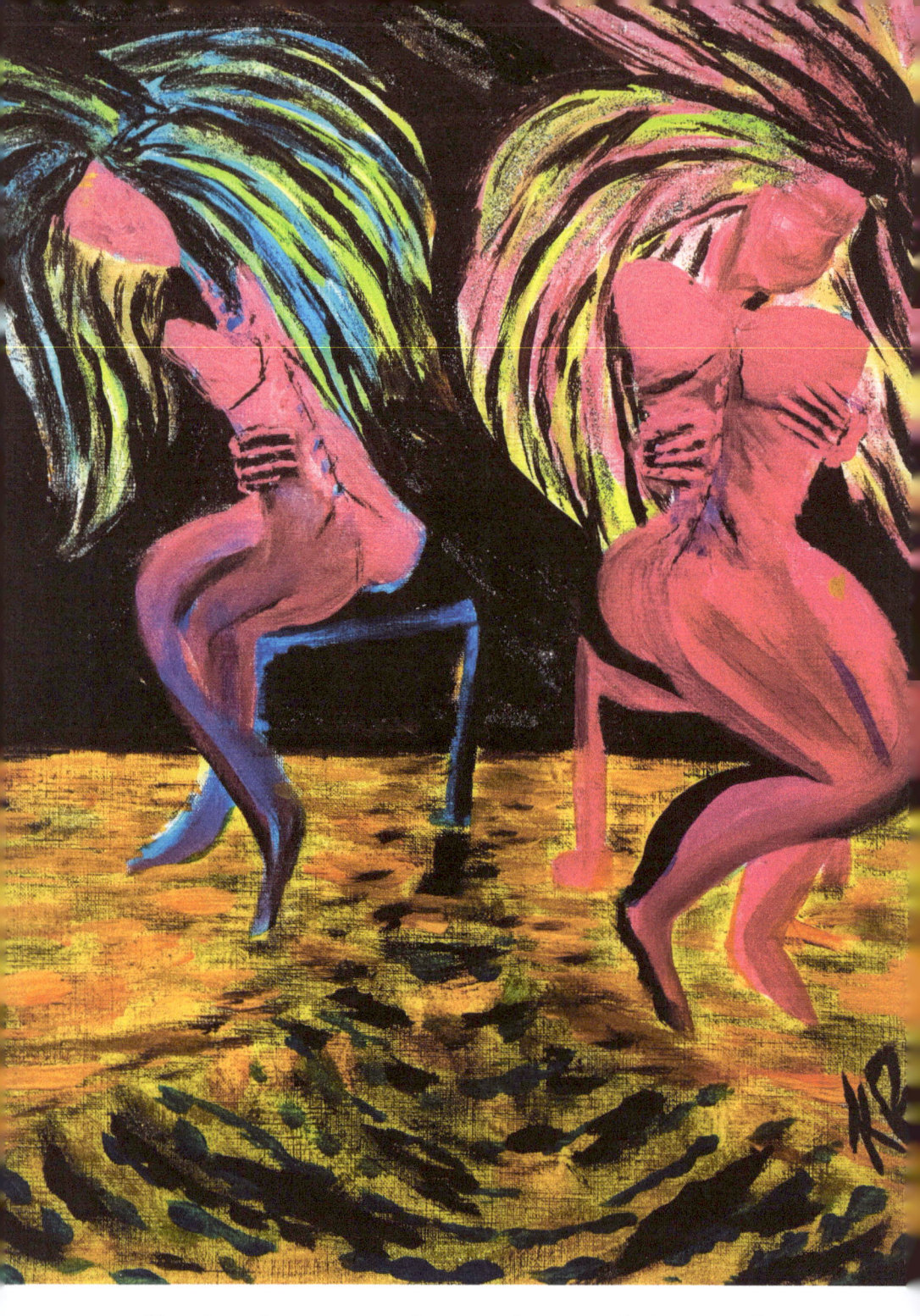

*She let the natural weirdness of things flow.*

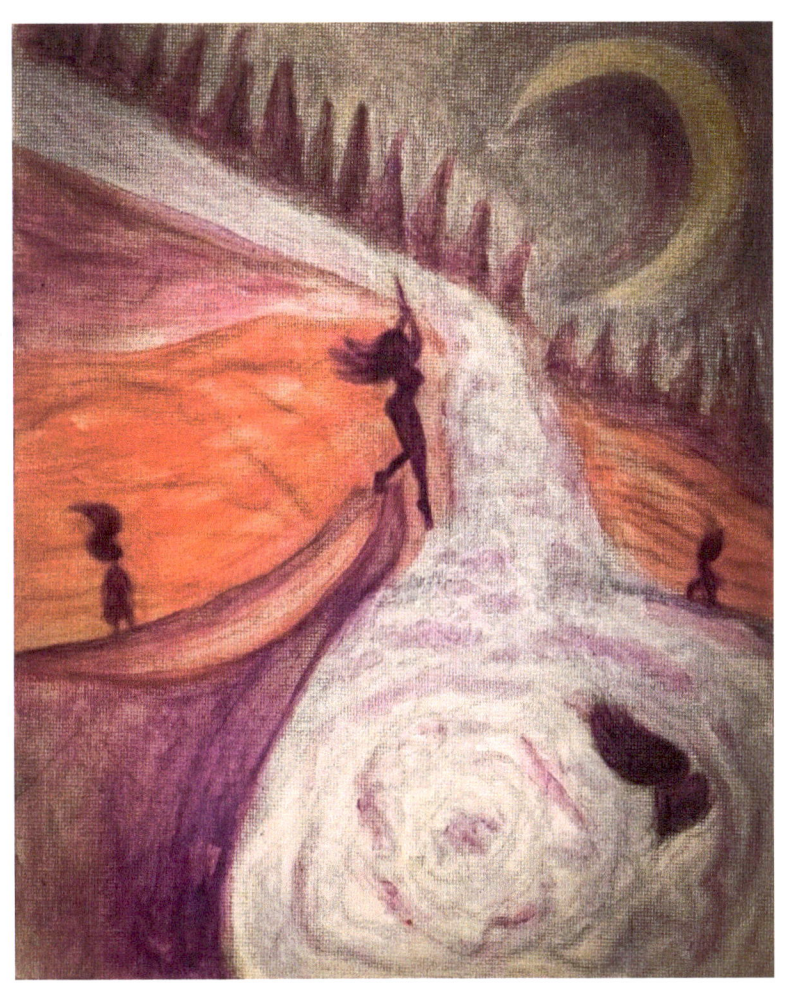

*She chose the right direction she would go.*

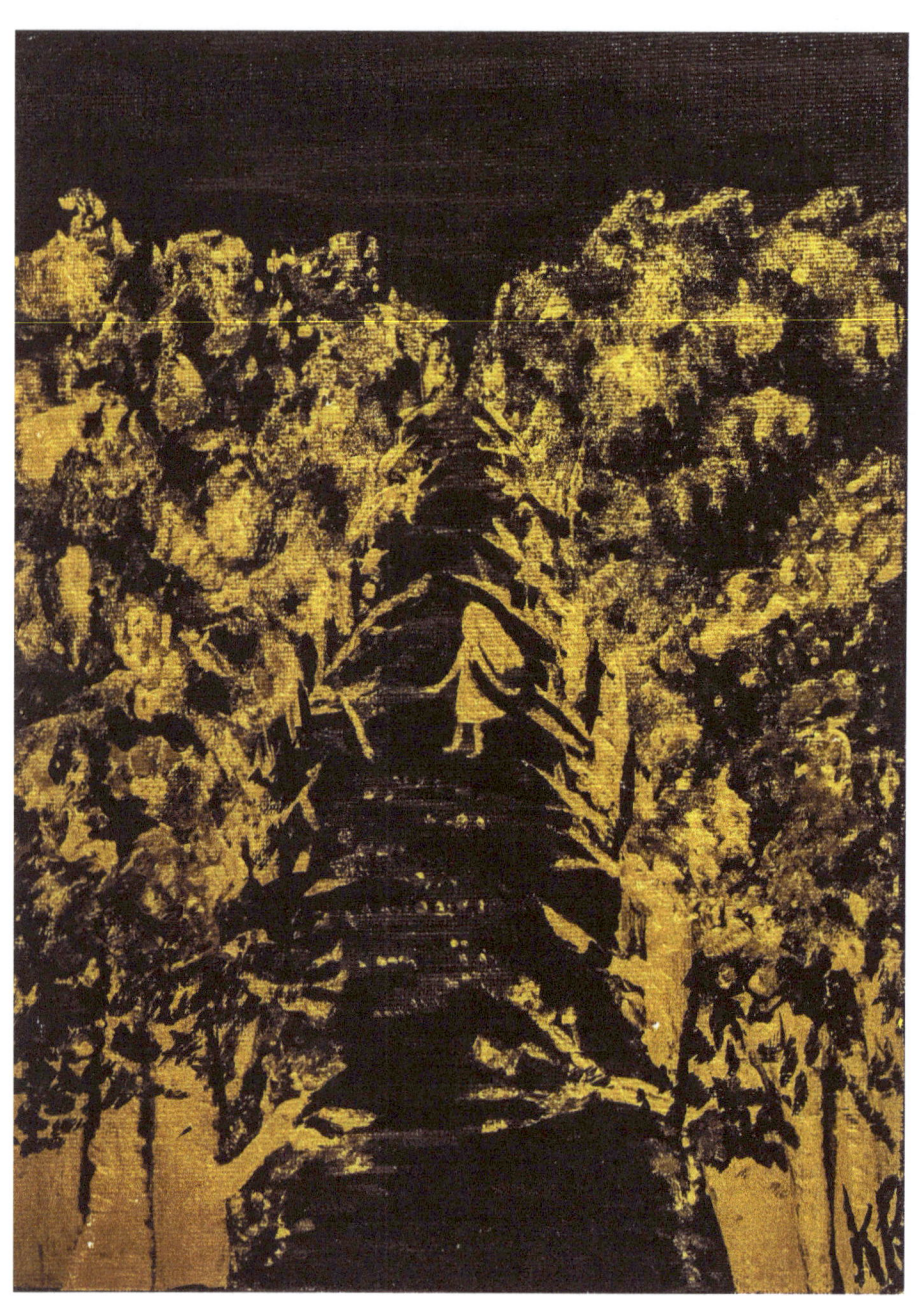

*She always encouraged happiness-*
*lonely or alone.*

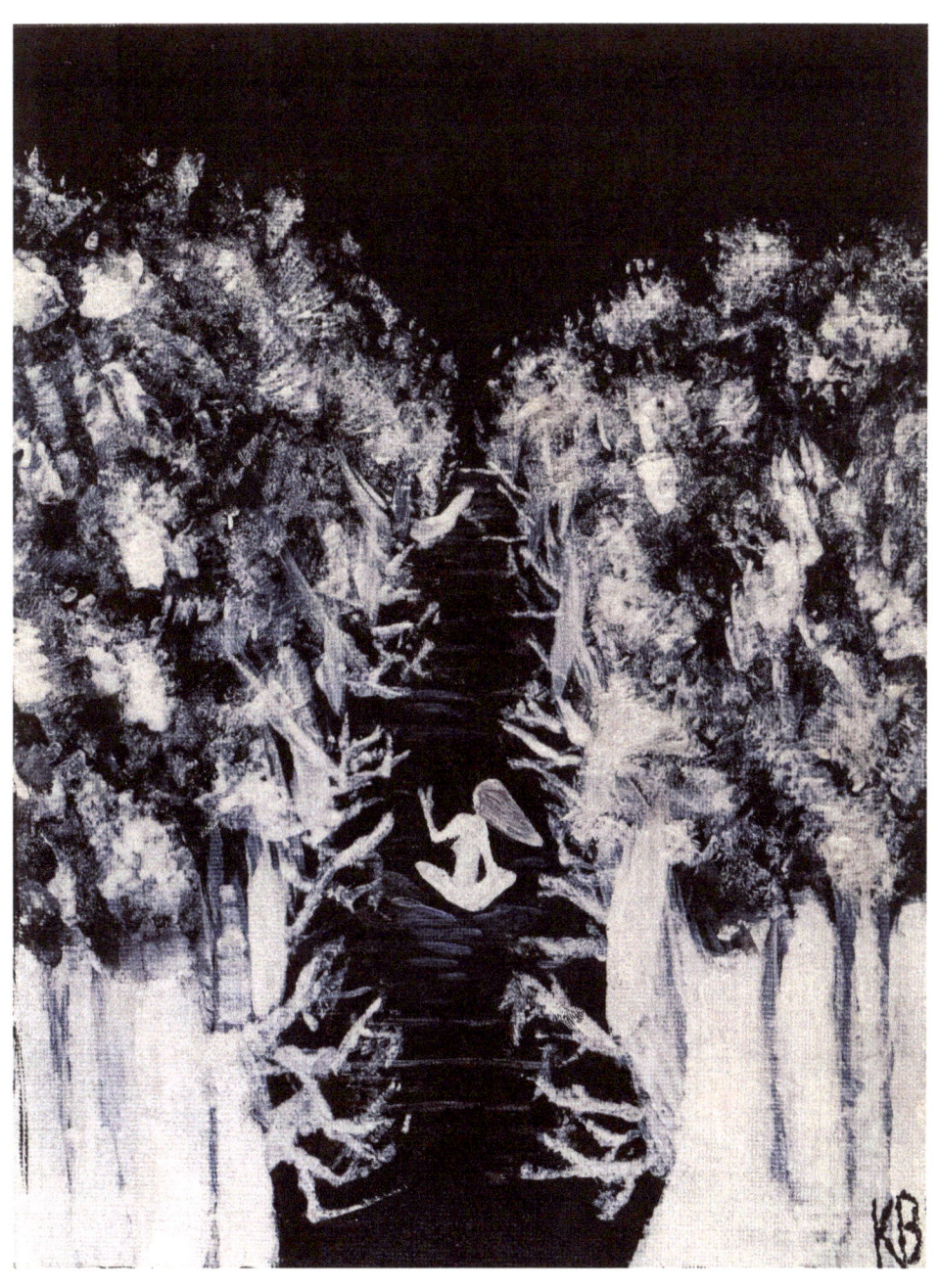

*She was optimistic; that was shown.*

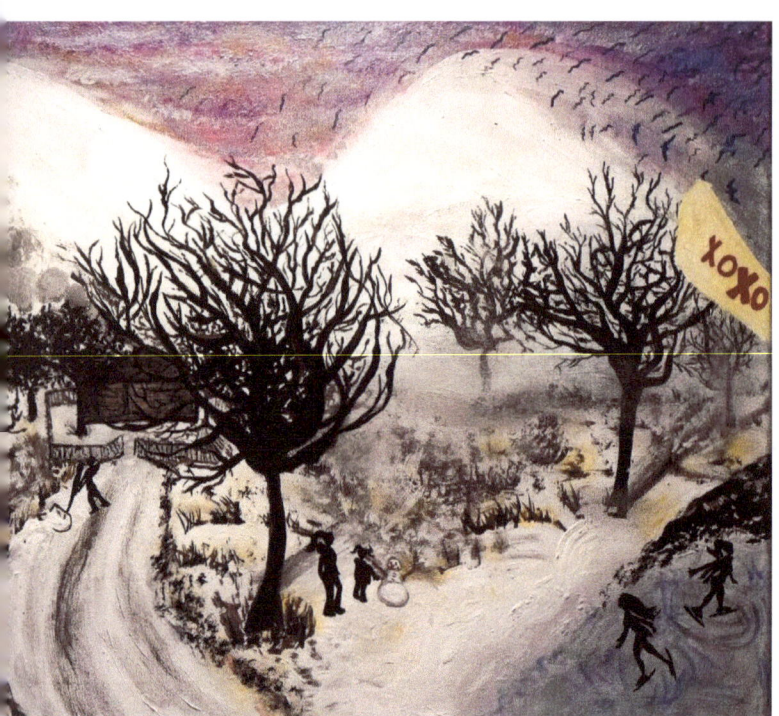

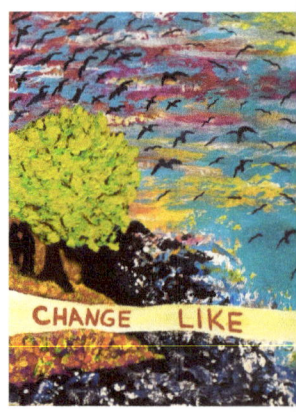

*She*
*changed*
*like the*
*seasons...*

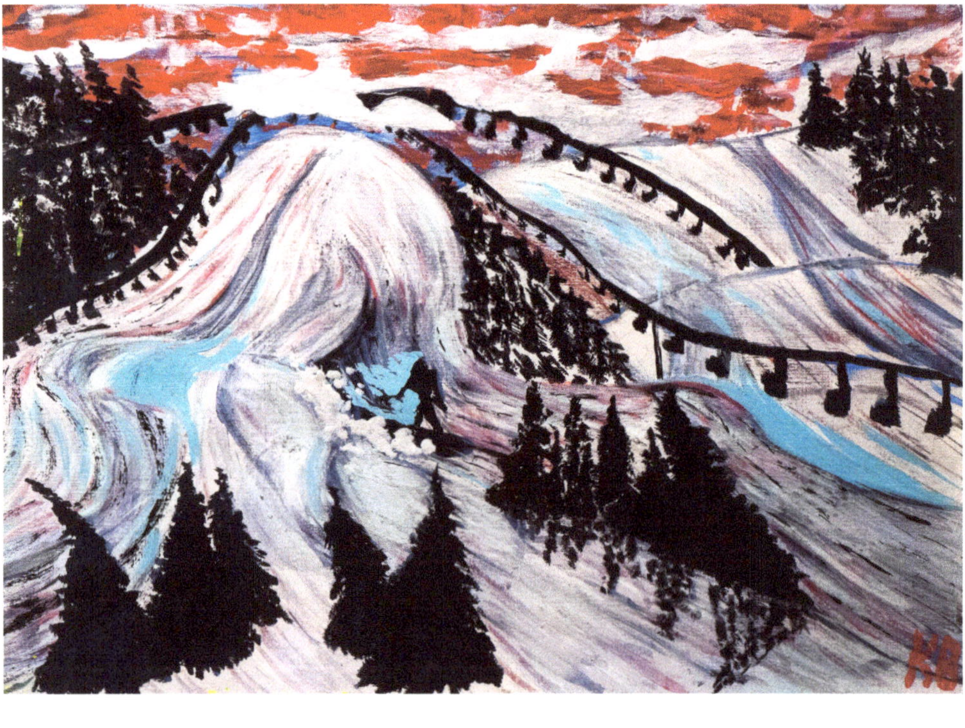

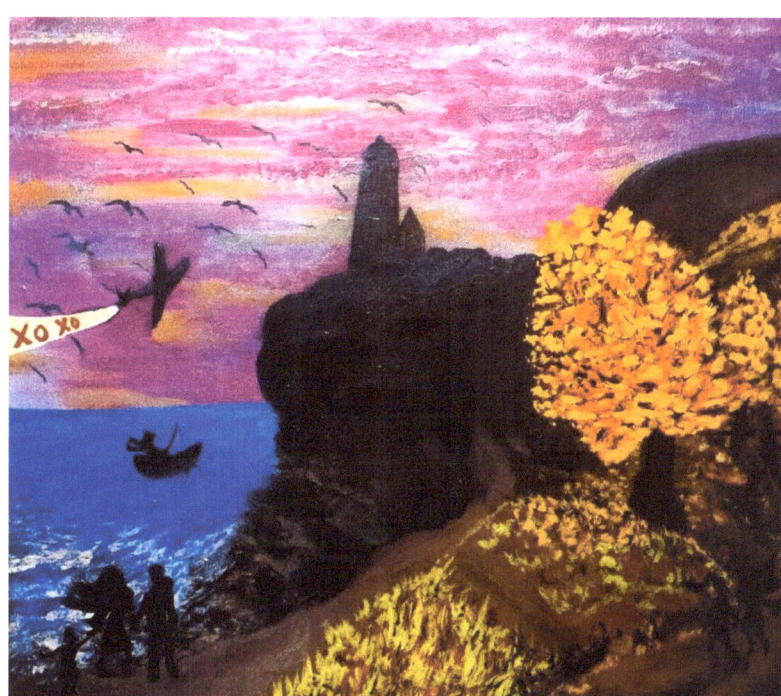

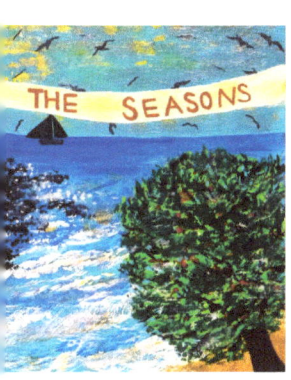

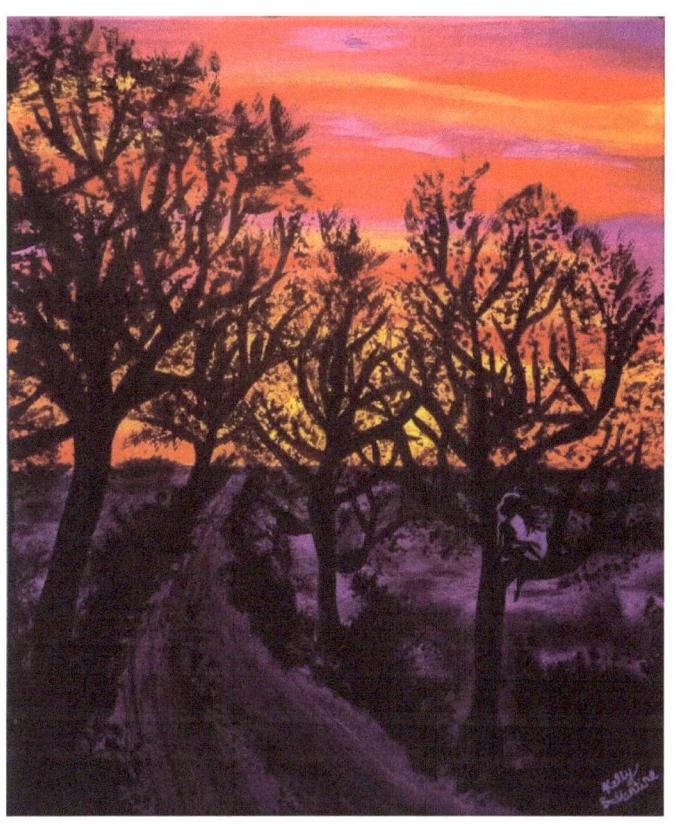

*If there
was a
natural or
necessary
reason.*

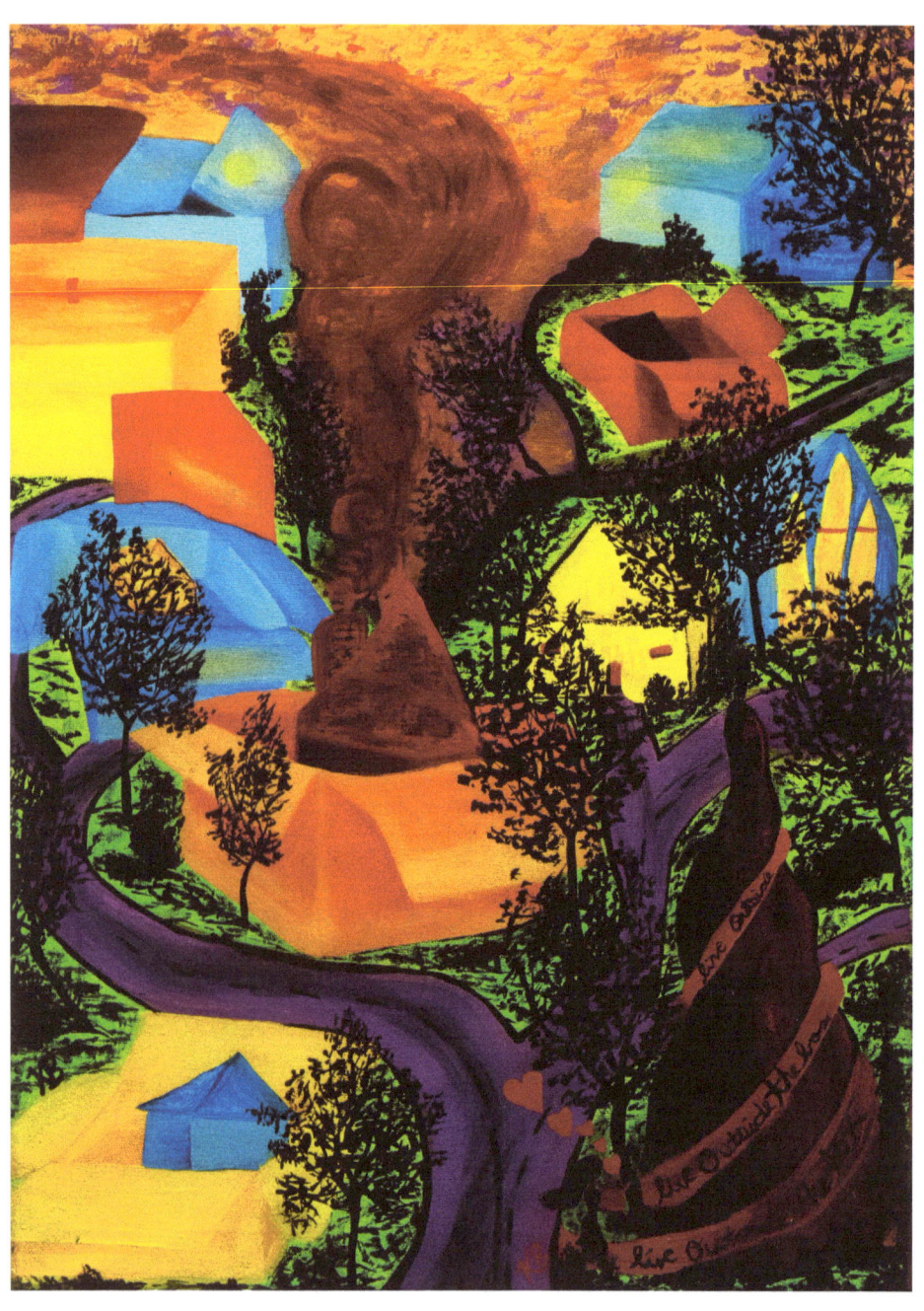

*She lived outside the box and created the world how she desired.*

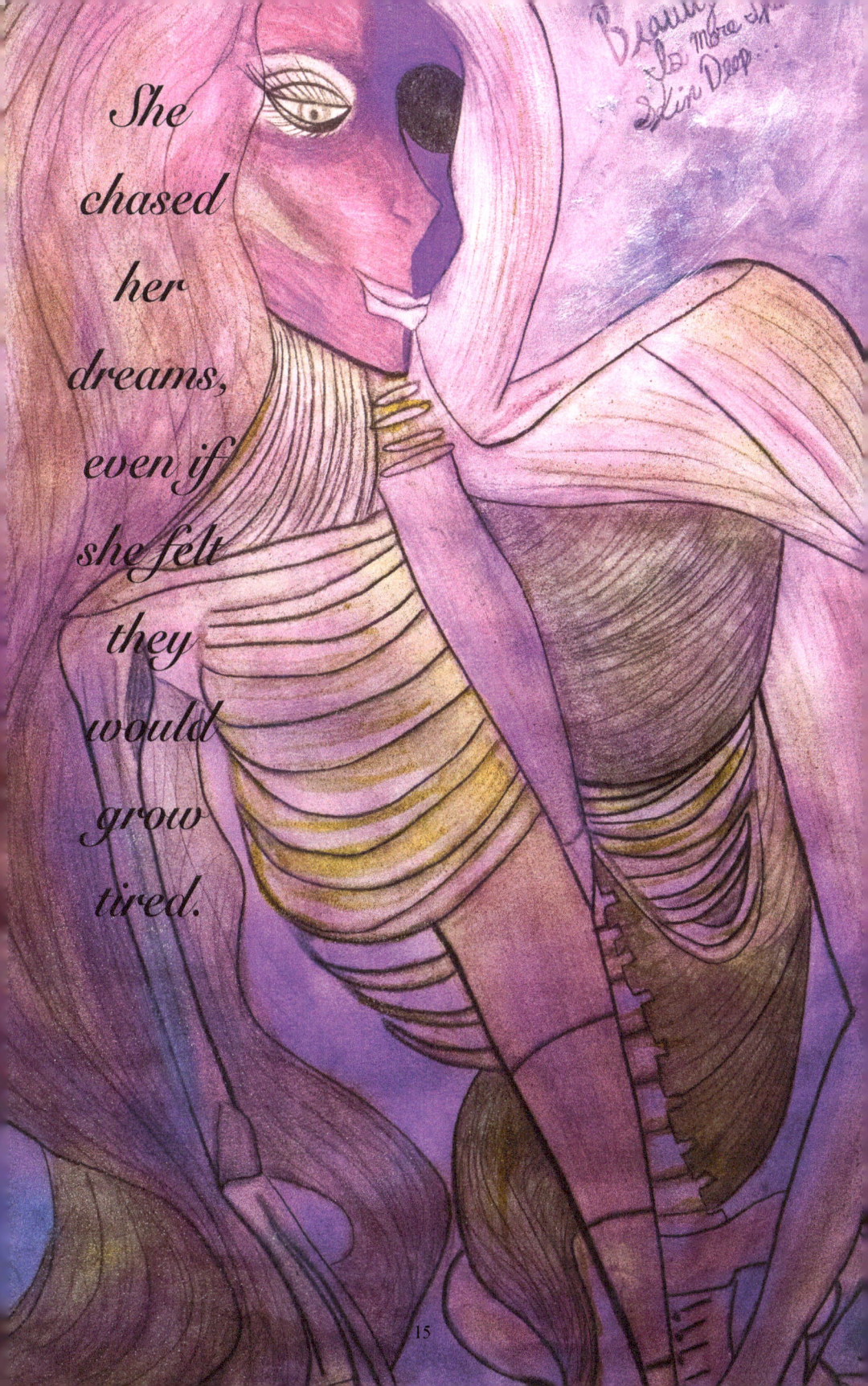

She

chased

her

dreams,

even if

she felt

they

would

grow

tired.

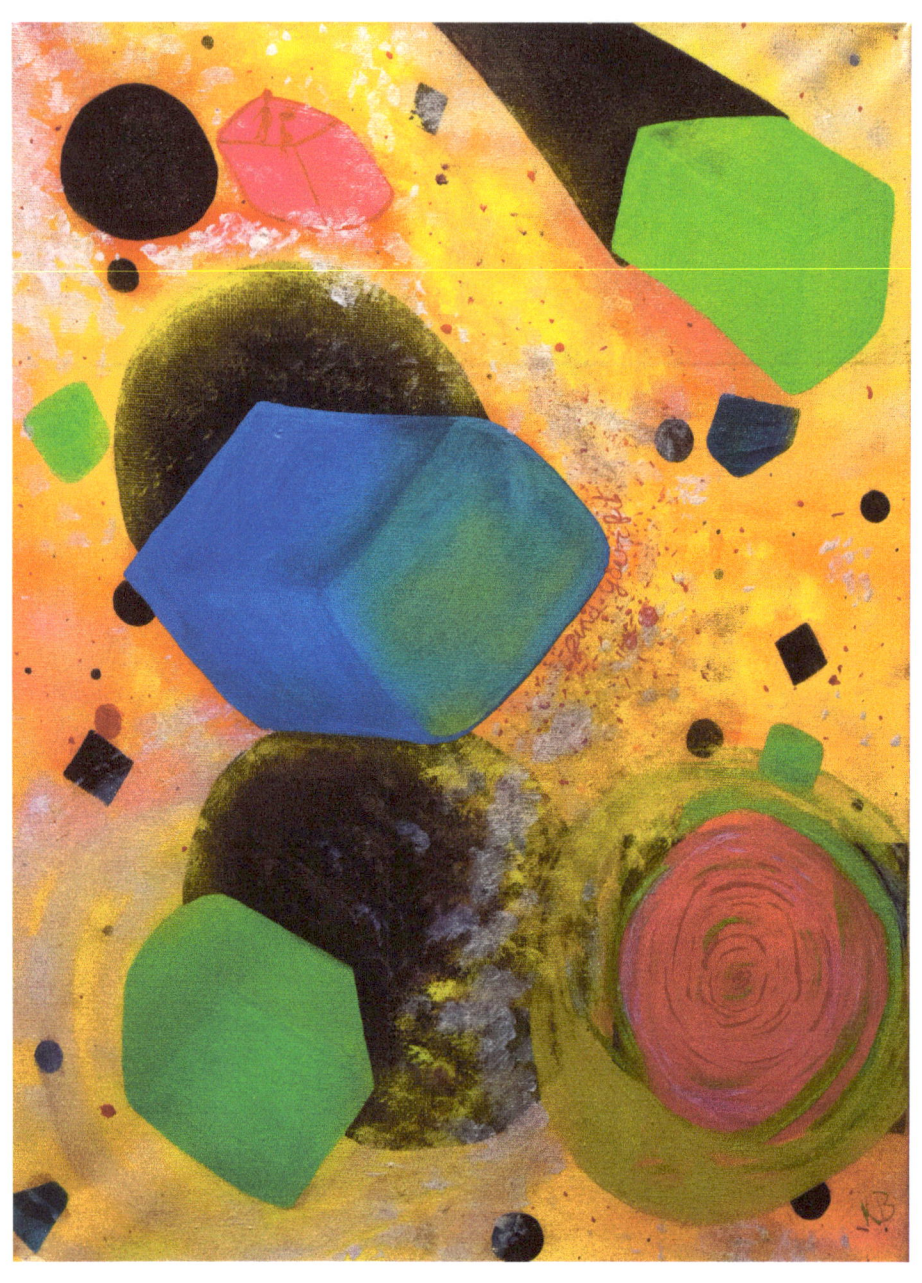

*She sent out her positive thoughts*
*and expectations.*

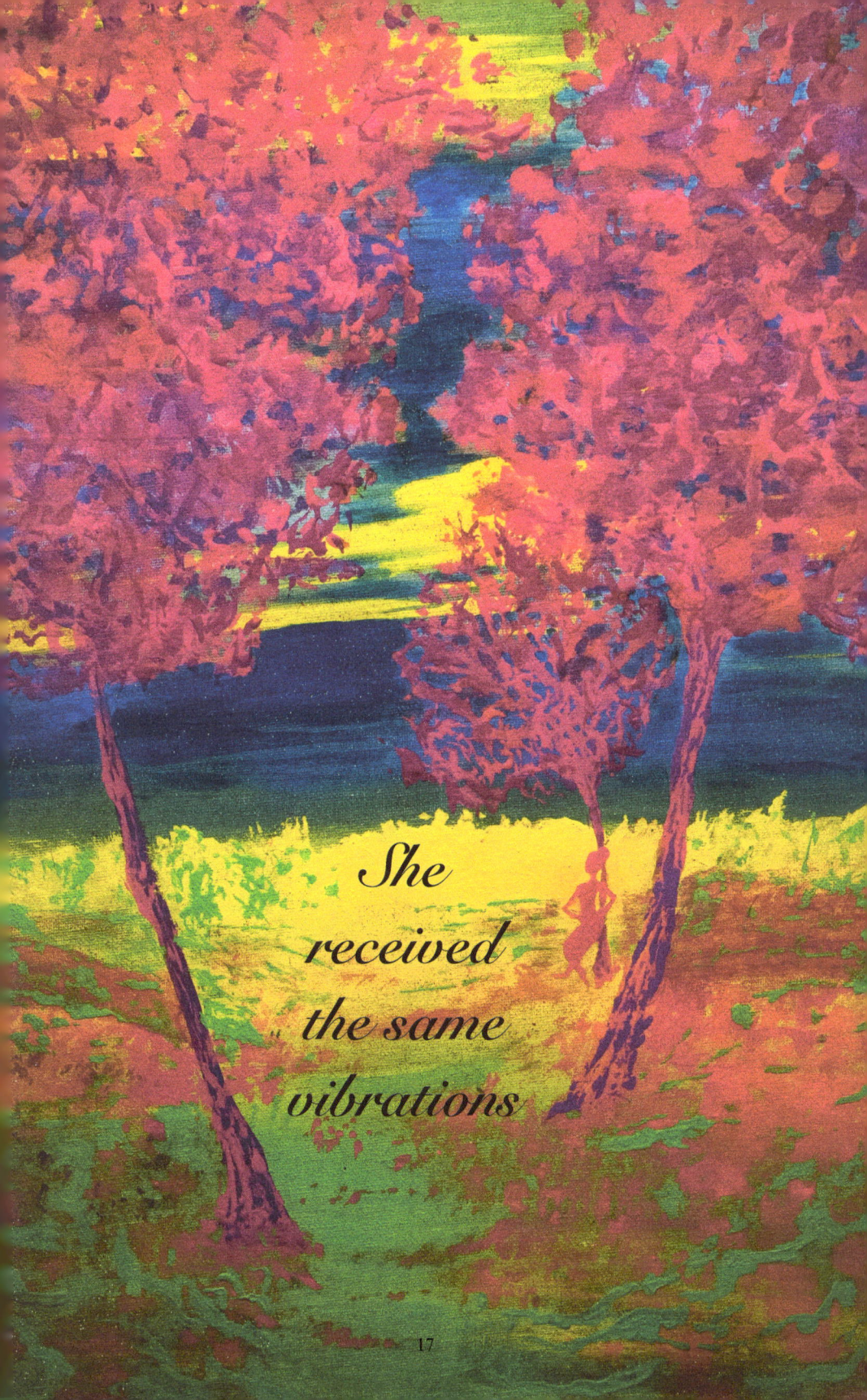

She received the same vibrations

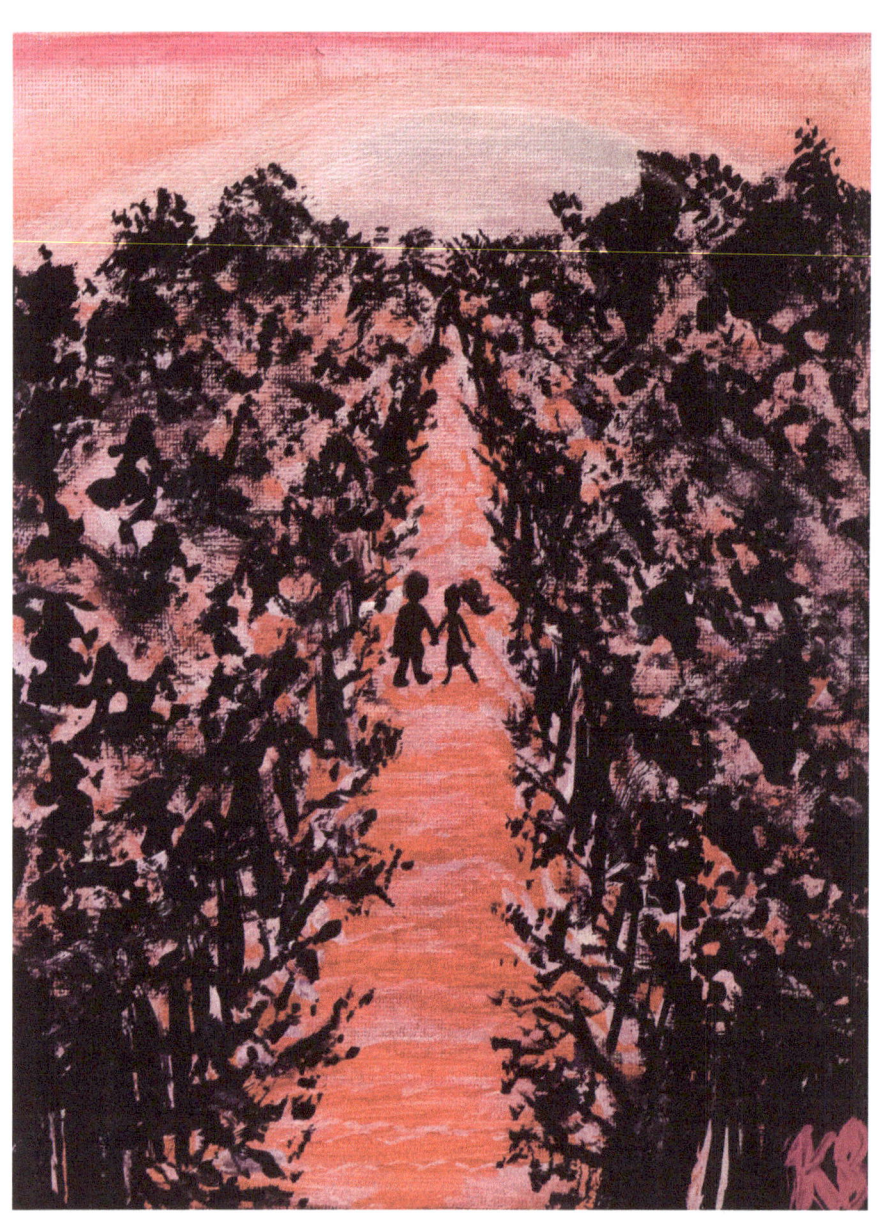

*She followed the feeling of love.*

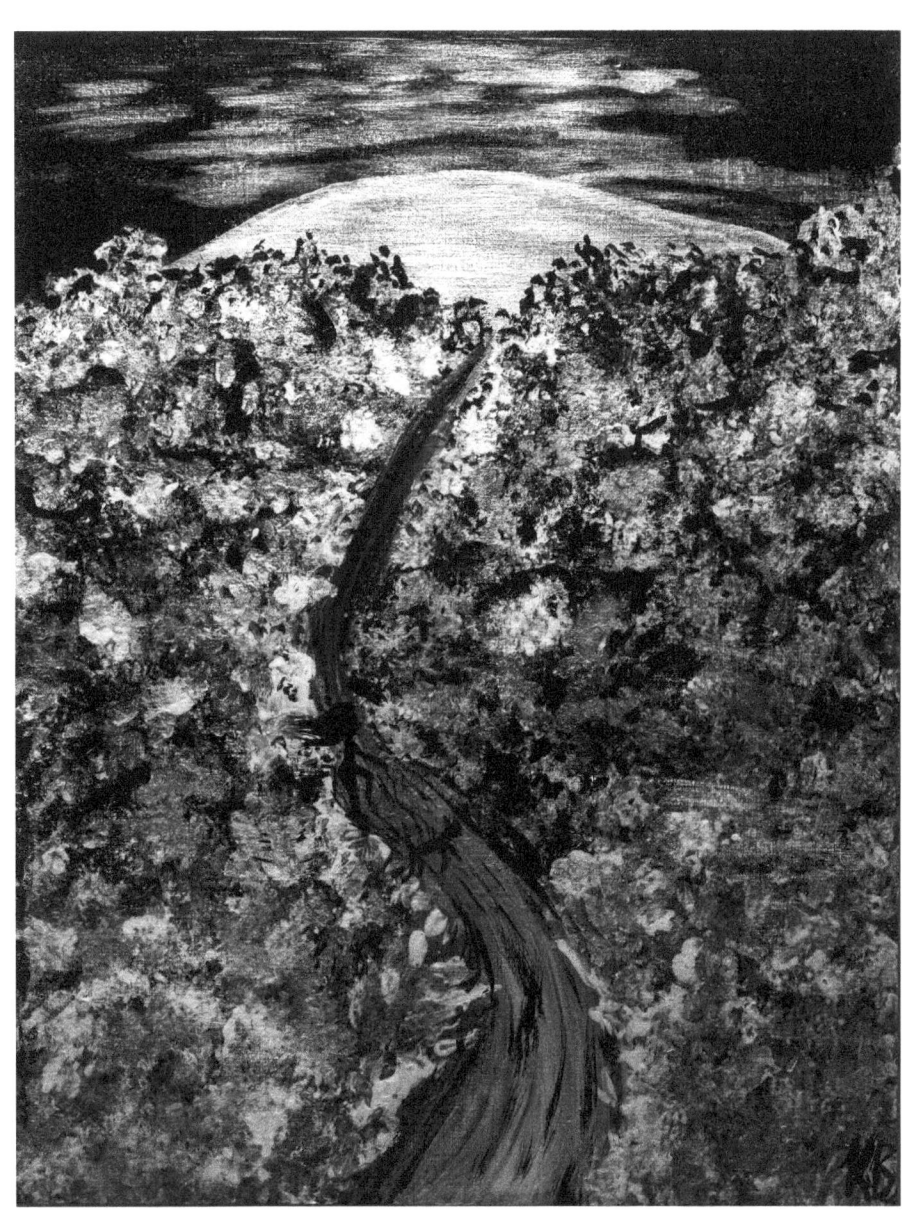

*She knew it would always rise above.*

# *Love*

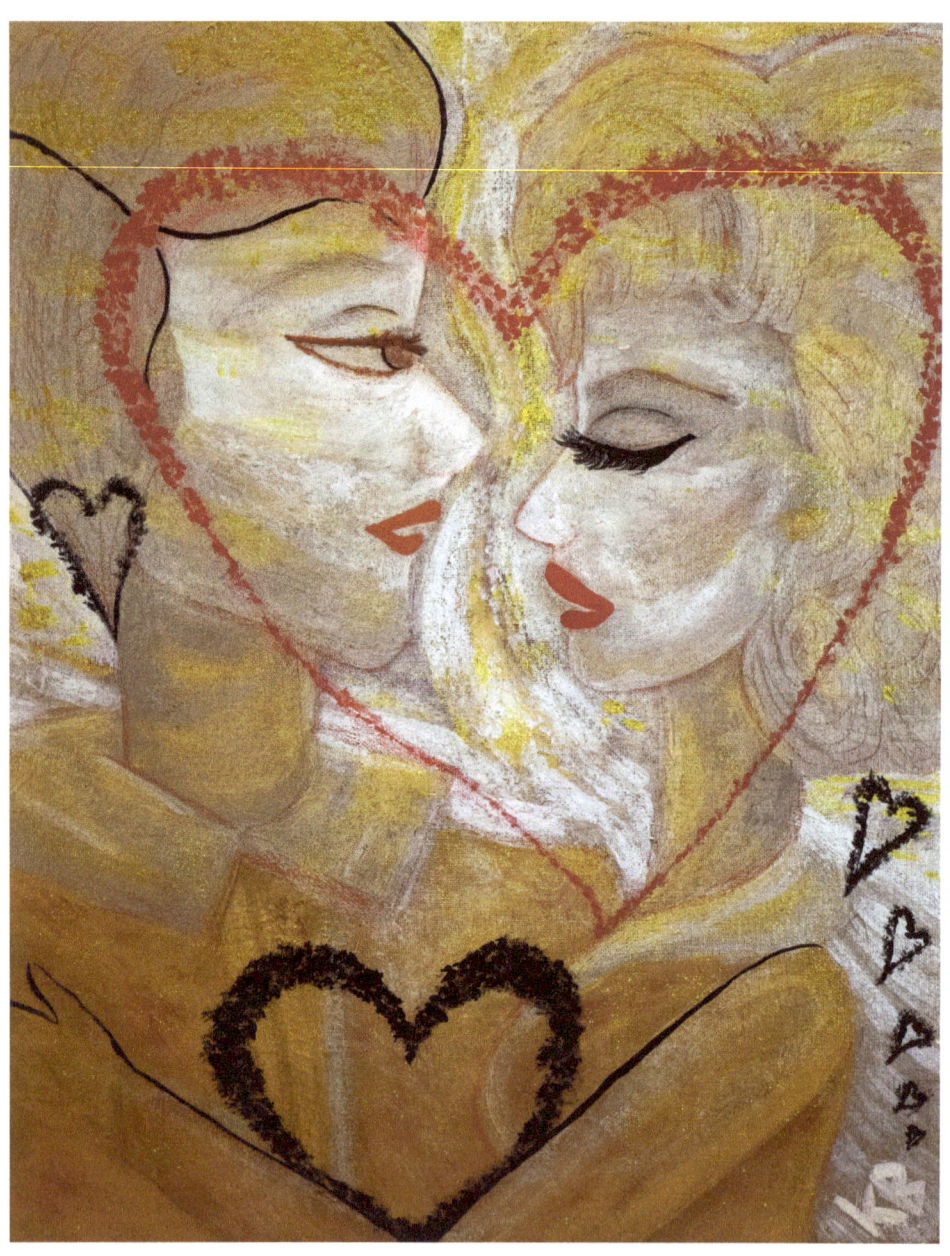

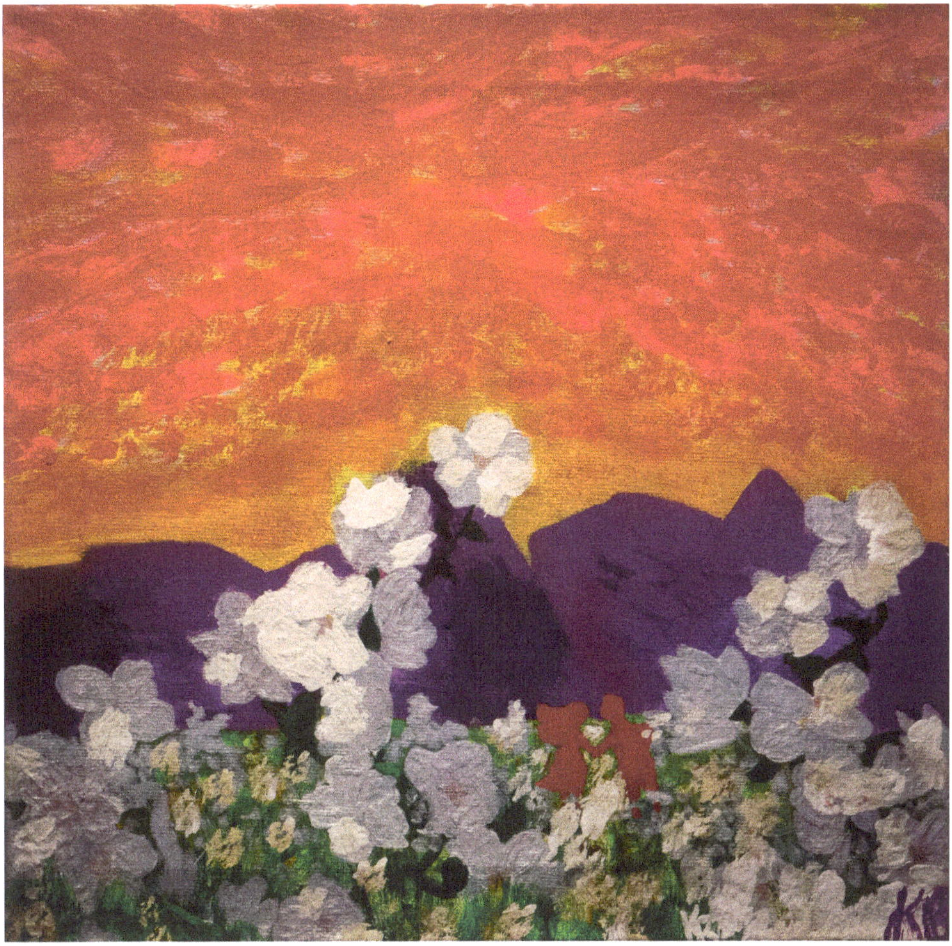

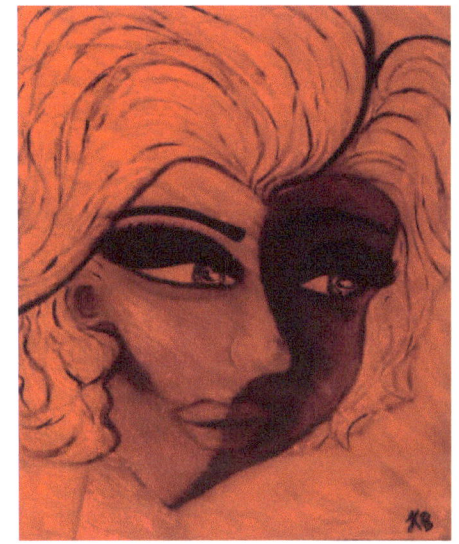

She gave her heart
out like it was
wealth but never
forgot to love
herself.

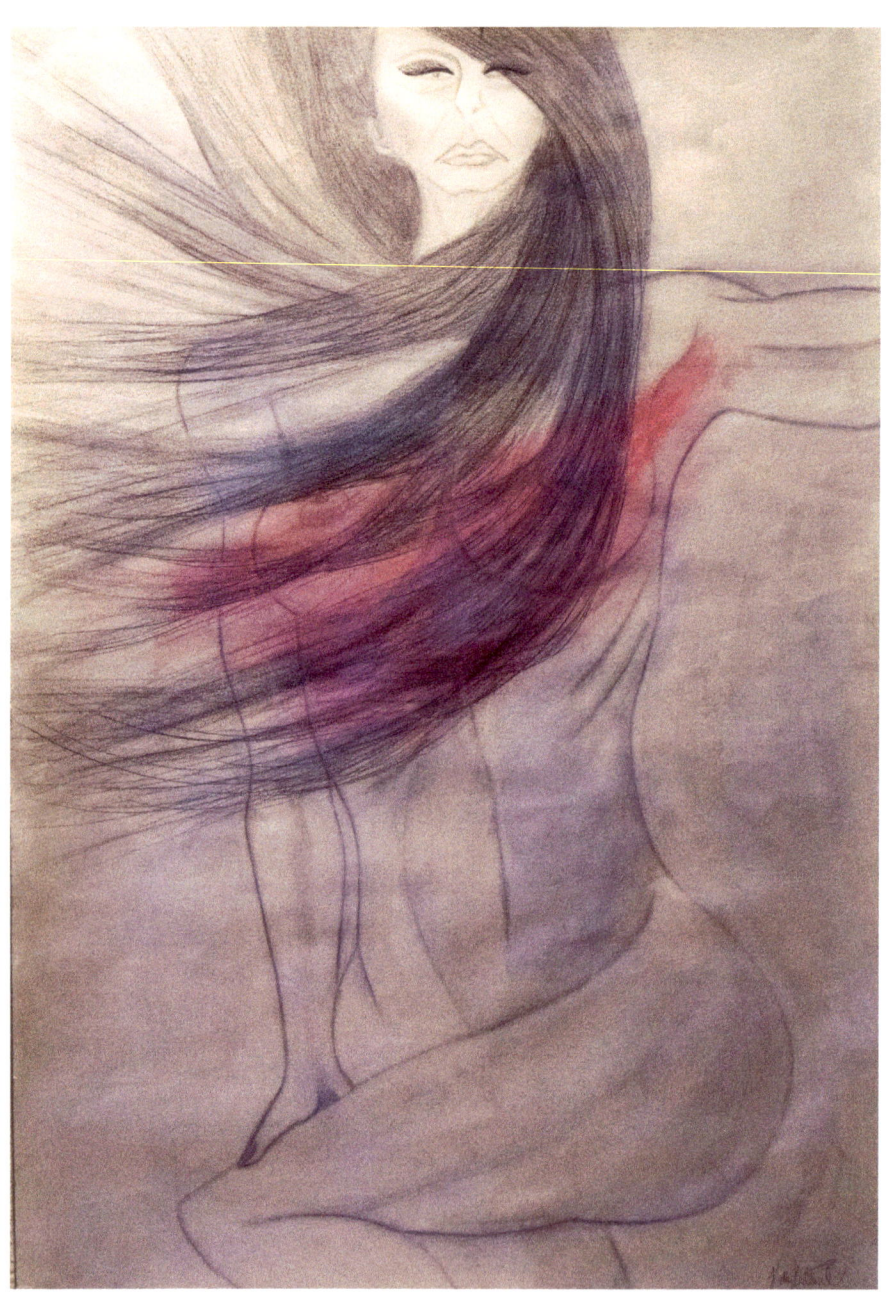

*To say the least...*

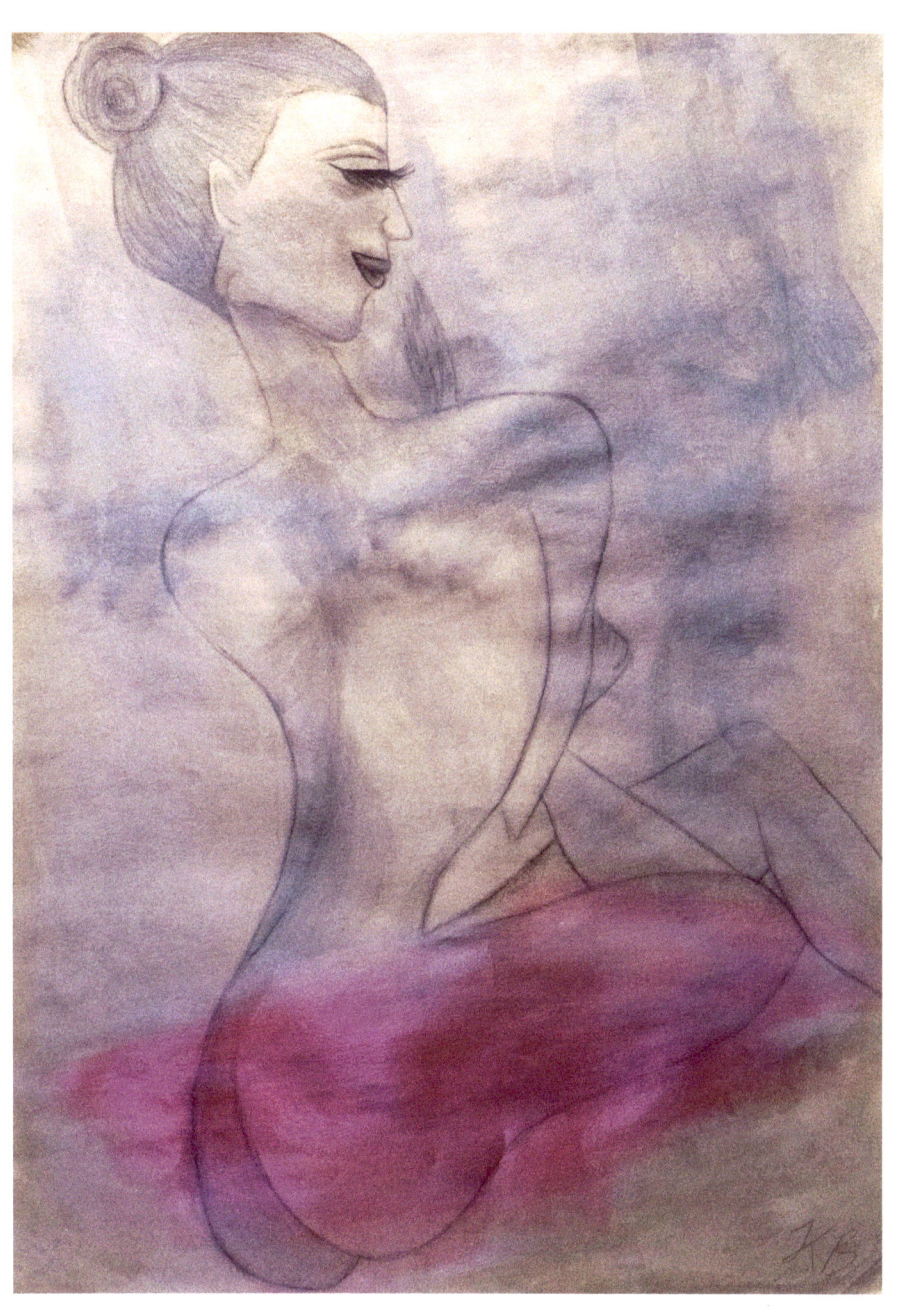

*She found peace.*

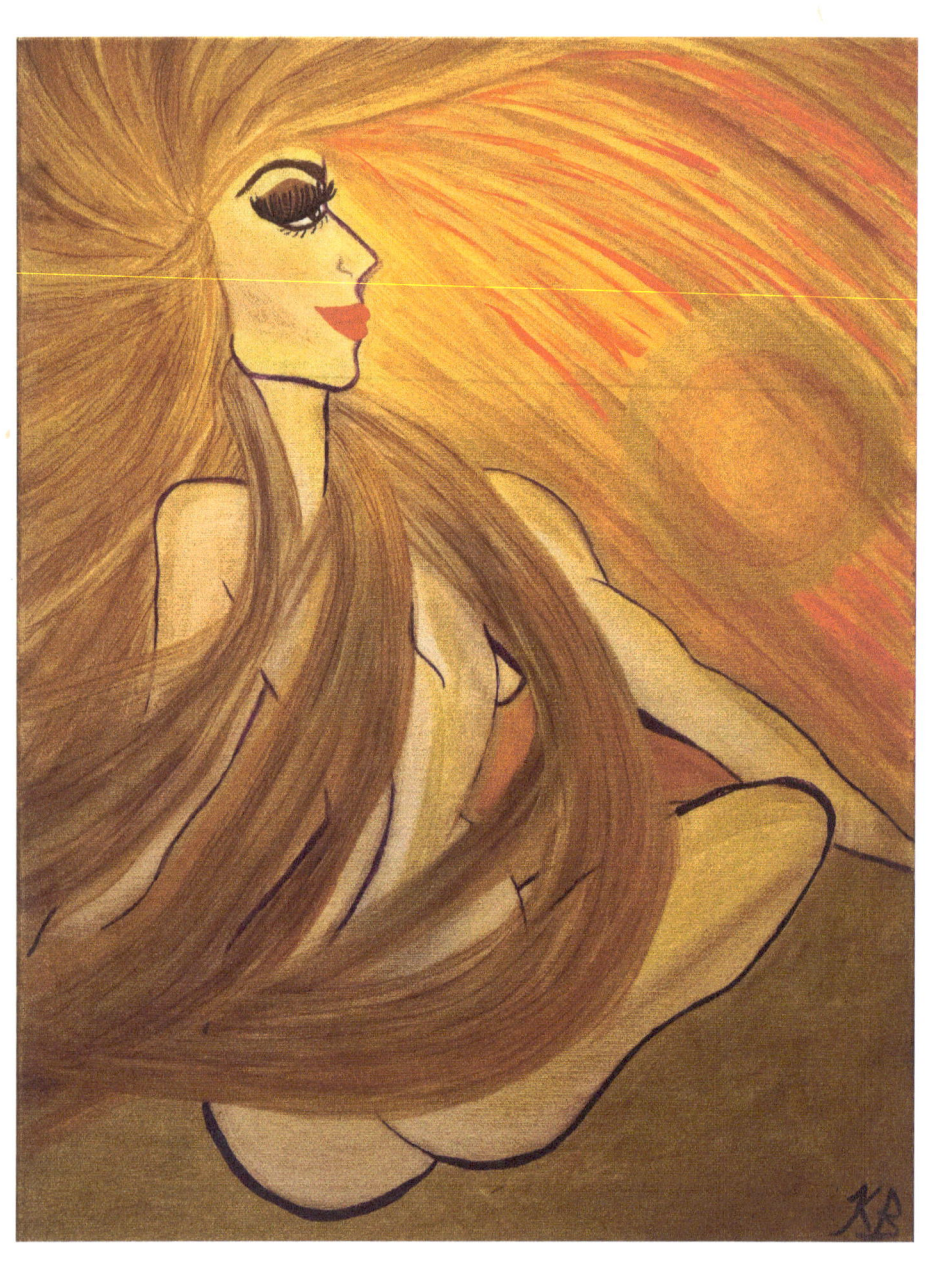

*She greeted each morning and night.*

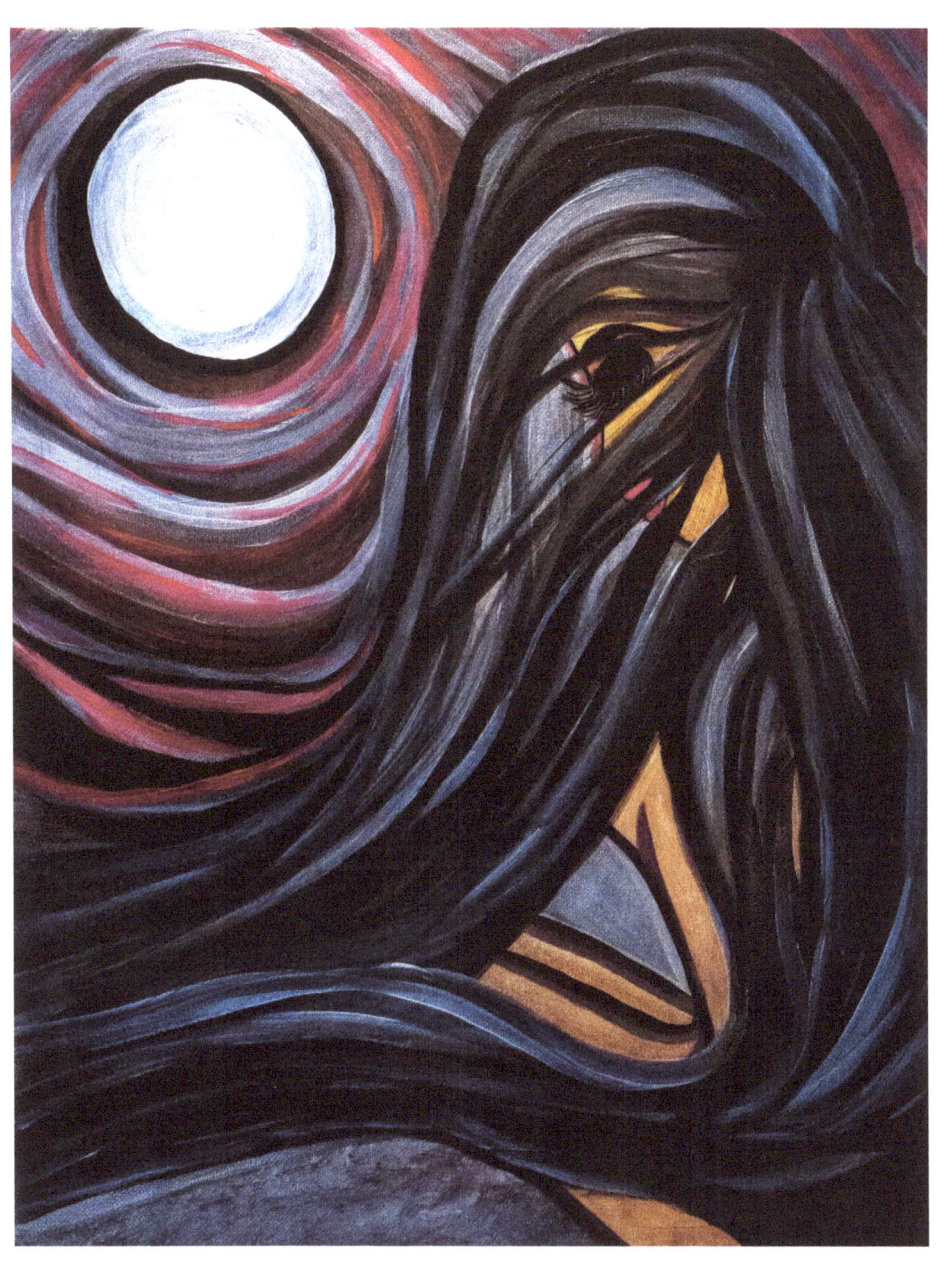

*She knew everything would be all right.*

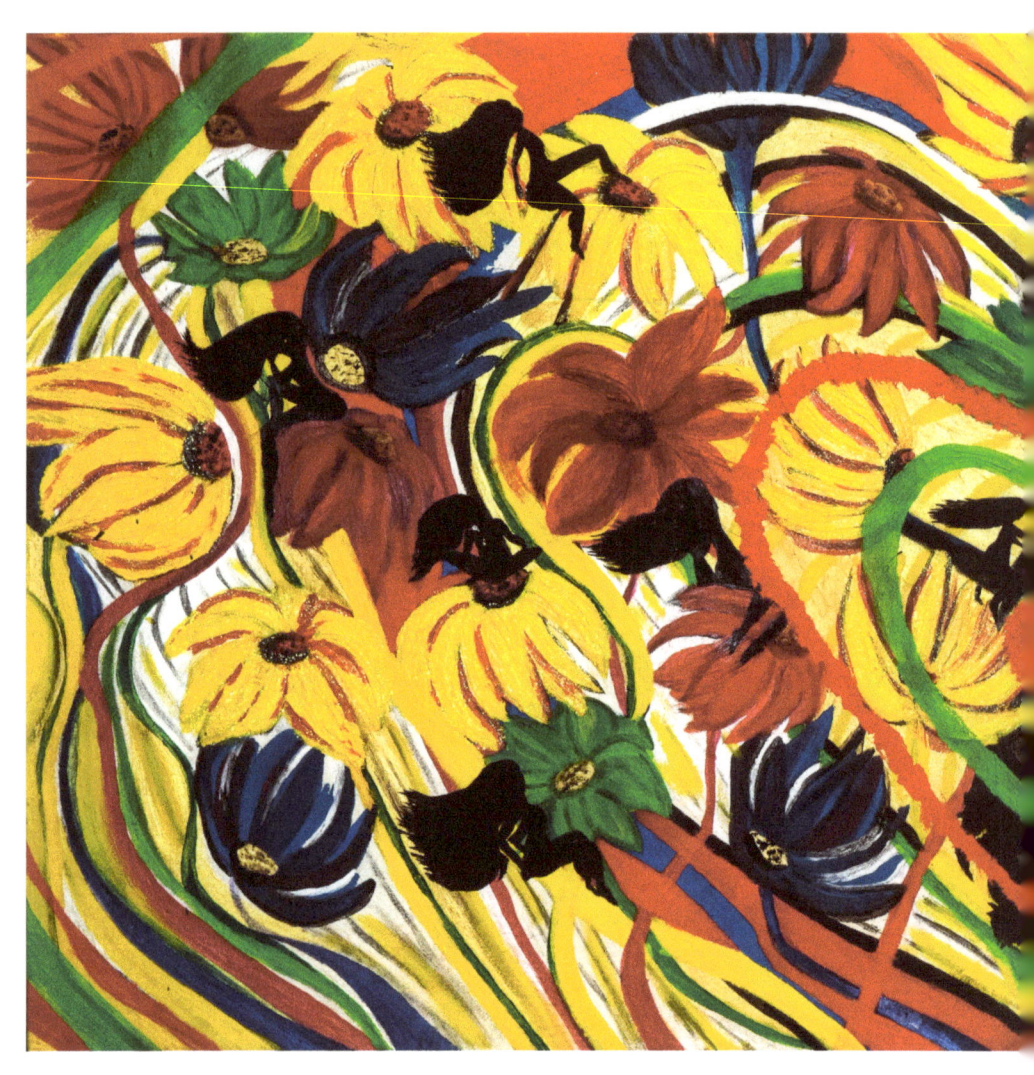

*She was a positive adapter.*

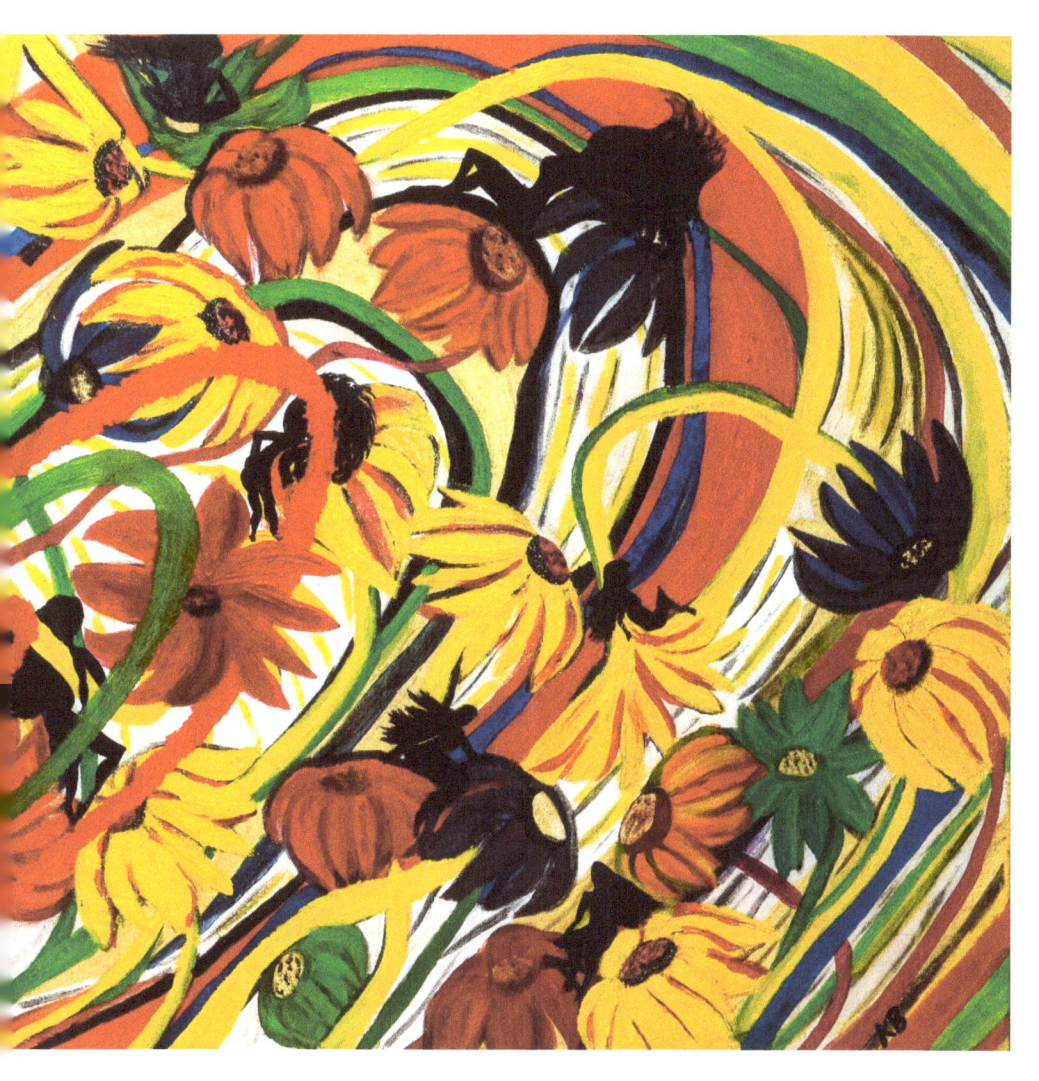

*She lived happily ever after.*

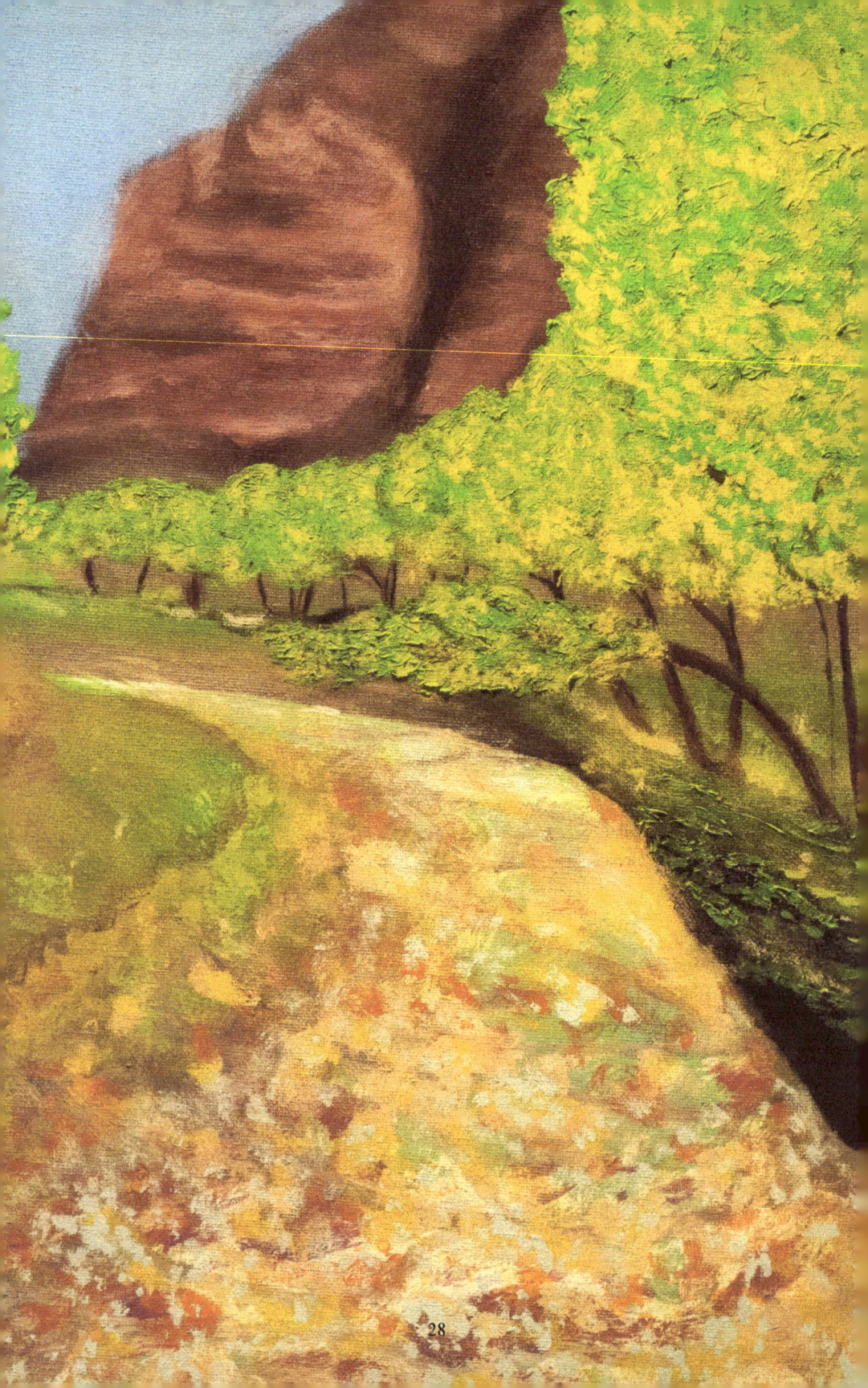

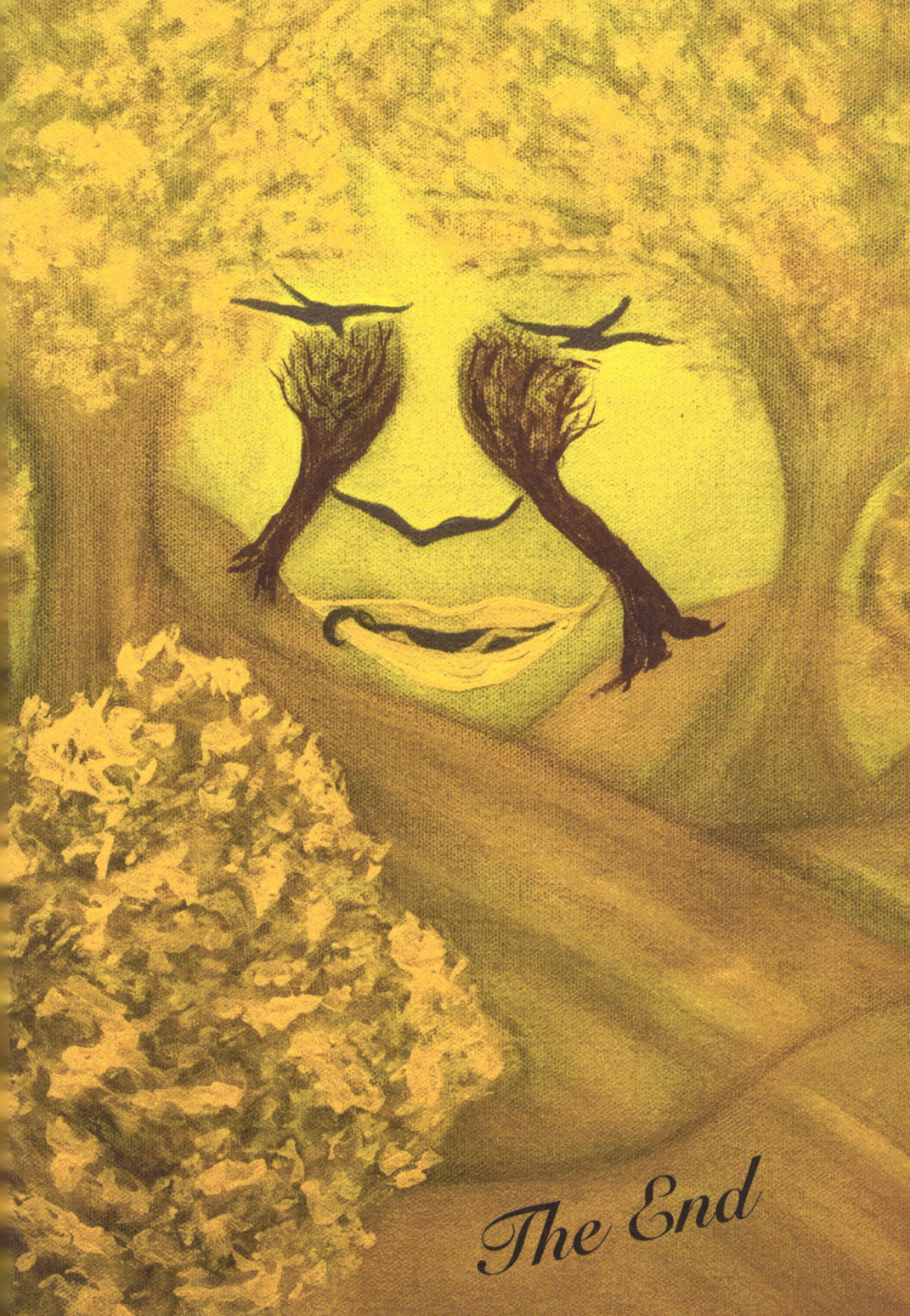

The End

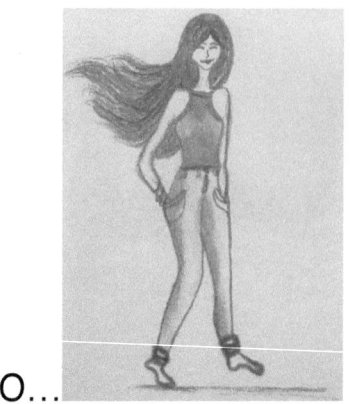

XO...

# Artist`s Statement

*I love art! I have always felt its
power to heal and inspire. I channel
my thoughts and feelings and invest
them into creativity and I make art!
Try to create and appreciate what
your fellow humans create. We are
all connected. Kindness inspires!
Art is freedom!*

*With Love,
Kelly Kristin Ballantine*

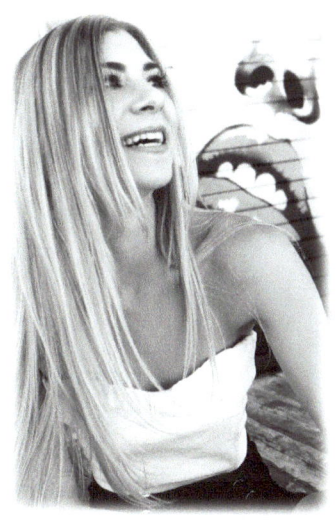

www.ingramcontent.com/pod-product-compliance
Lightning Source LLC
Chambersburg PA
CBHW041611180526
45159CB00002BC/810